Benedict XVI
Thoughts on St Paul

On the occasion of the "Pauline Year"

Edited by Lucio Coco

*All booklets are published thanks to the
generous support of the members of the
Catholic Truth Society*

CATHOLIC TRUTH SOCIETY
PUBLISHERS TO THE HOLY SEE

Contents

Preface 3

Introduction 6

Apostolic Vocation 12

Encounter with Jesus .19

Life in the Spirit 31

Christian Experience .39

Church of God 56

Sacraments 73

Pray Unceasingly 82

Preface

By celebrating the Pauline Year we intend to put at the centre of our reflections the figure of Paul. Remembering Paul two thousand years after his birth calls us to reflect deeply on his figure. Paul's journey on the road to Damascus carries the significance of a true spiritual journey. In a certain sense, it reproduces the experience of every person who has ever been freed from illusions and dreams in order to find authenticity. Paul calls this decisive experience "vocation". He is aware that his conversion is not the result of a train of thought or reflection, but the fruit of an unpredictable divine grace. It is of primary importance to recognize that it is God who initiates this first step. This, in turn, frees us from any kind of sterile "activism" to place ourselves under his love, his *caritas*. Thus we are freely given the space to nurture our vocation and love.

The road to Damascus is also a place of encounter, an encounter with Jesus. Jesus comes near to that man who until then had ignored him and did not recognize him: just as often occurs with us in our personal histories. The two disciples on the road to Emmaus also experienced this. The circumstances do not change. It is always Jesus who approaches the distracted or incredulous person, as in Paul's case.

After this encounter the life of any person cannot be but transformed. Paul's life shows precisely this. It is a continuous witness of this encounter, always needing to refer to Jesus, to center his life on him, to learn from him.

Paul's spiritual journey has a third aspect: that of the mission. His task will be to bring the name of the Lord "before all peoples, kings and the children of Israel" (*Ac* 9:15). Bearing Christ; whoever has met Christ, and has entered into contact with him, isn't able to keep him to himself. We can think of the joyous journey of Mary to Elizabeth. The mission awaits us on the return from Damascus: to share and communicate the experience of love, of God's grace, and the joy of Christ who has revealed himself to us and has come to us on the roads (not always easy) of the world. The proclamation of the mission contains in itself also the revelation of the cross: "I will show him – says the Lord – how much he must suffer fro my name" (*Ac* 9:16). The cross tells us that our manner of giving ourselves for others should be that of Jesus. He gave himself for us, giving up any type of privilege, emptying himself and choosing to serve. Also Saint Paul carried this cross in his life, full of passion for Jesus, suffering pain even unto his martyrdom in Rome.

I hope the reflections collected in this book may accompany many readers through a similar spiritual journey: that their life may be authentically transformed by their encounter with Jesus, just as Paul's life was transformed.

Tarcisio Cardinal Bertone
Secretary of State to His Holiness

Introduction

Pope Bendict XVI announced the induction of a new jubilee year to commemorate the second millennium since Paul's birth, from June 28, 2008 to June 29 2009. He encouraged activities that favored a re-awakening of Pauline spirituality, such as "liturgical, cultural and ecumenical events" and "pastoral and social visits". Together with a call for conventions of an academic nature he encouraged "special publications about the texts of Paul, that will serve to make ever more known the immense riches of the teaching enclosed therein" (*Homily*, 28.6.07).

This booklet follows on from the Holy Father's proposal. Its purpose is to provide readers of Paul with the Pope's particular viewpoint on this extraordinary witness of faith in Christ's redeeming role for humanity, through a collection of his own reflections.

"How does the encounter between a human being and Christ take place?" (*Catechesis*, 25.10.06): this question is the starting point for Pope Benedict's reading of St Paul. His answer is of help in making explicit the contours not only of Paul's faith in Christ, but those of every Christian. While reflecting on Paul's conversion, Benedict underlines the fact that it was not the result of reasoning, or merely human logic, but the fruit of divine intervention, "an unpredictable divine grace" (*ibidem*). Thus, Paul's case puts before us from the outset "this not seeking oneself, but receiving oneself from Christ" (*Catechesisi* 8.11.06) that represents the primary characteristic of Christian identity. Before his conversion "he had not been a man far from God and his Law" (*ibidem*), but "an observant Jew, such a faithful observance as to lead to fanaticism". In the light of his meeting with Christ, Paul understood that he had tried to build himself up alone, with his own justice. ...

Paul's life, beginning with his vocation on the road to Damascus, witnesses also another decision and resolution: that of making Christ the centre of one's life. This "gift of oneself with Christ", participating "personally in the very life of Christ", constitutes the other element of Christian identity that Paul propounded in his life and teachings. To place Christ at the centre of one's existence is to mark our lives with " the encounter and communion with him and his Word" (*Catechesis*, 25.10.06). For Paul "it isn't enough to say that Christians are those who are baptized or who believe; for him it is just as important to say that they are 'in Christ Jesus'" (*Catechesis*, 8.11.06). Paul says "Christ is in you/us" (*Rm* 8:10; 2 *Co* 13:5). Pope Benedict notes that this element of mutual compenetration of Christ and the Christian has an almost mystical connotation. That is why, just as Christ became a man, we must become incarnate in Christ and enter his feelings "of mercy, goodness, humility, meekness, patience" (*Col* 3:12). In this way we become his disciples by being ready to bear and forgive, and his imitators in being able to love.

Pope Benedict constantly invites us to imitate Paul. He calls to mind Paul's own exhortation to become imitators of him, just as he imitates Christ (*Catechesis*, 25.10.06). The incarnate Word has the power to transform human existence from within. With the life-giving action of his Spirit he can elevate humanity to the dignity of children of God (*Rm* 8:14-17). Benedict explains: "This is our great dignity: that of not merely being an image, but children of God" (*Catechesis*, 15.22.06). The presence of the Spirit in our hearts is a guarantee and certitude of this divine adoption that distinguishes us from slaves, "unable to do otherwise". It gives us back the freedom of children and heirs (*Rm* 8:17) who feel responsible for the inheritance entrusted to them by their father. This contrasts superficial freedoms, often merely freedoms of choice that are extinguished rapidly. By reflecting on this passage Pope Benedict presents an important lesson for today: that freedom and responsibility go

Introduction

hand in hand, and that "true freedom is manifested through responsibility, in a course of action that assumes co-responsibility for the world, for oneself and for others" (*Homily*, 3.6.06).

We may list but a few of the themes that the Holy Father tackles in this great catechesis on Saint Paul: the centrality of Christ; adoption to sonship through the Spirit; the Church as the depository of the mystery of Christ ("the body of Christ" as Paul says); the passages about baptism and the Eucharist that reflect intensely on communion with Christ and being in Christ; priesthood "understood as bringing God to human beings" (*Speech*, 22.12.06); the life of prayer necessary to scrutinize God's will (*Homily*, 25.1.08); the quest for holiness as the realization "of what we already are through the elevation to the dignity of sons and daughters of God, brought by Christ (*angelus*, 1.11.05). These constitute a principal element of the Holy Father's magisterium. Not by chance did he visit the Basilica of Saint Paul Outside the Walls immediately following his election to the pontificate. There he put under the auspices of this tireless apostle of Christ all of his action as pastor of the Universal Church. On that occasion he reminded us of how he had been inspired by Saint Paul himself "to make Christ the centre of his life, leaving everything behind for the sublimity of knowing him and his mystery of love, and committing himself to proclaim him to everyone, especially the pagans 'to the glory of his name' (*Rm* 1,5)" (*Homily*, 24.4.05). It is these words that we desire to expound in this brief presentation. His words are able to condense within a short sentence the essential lesson of Paul to "restart with Christ" and "not place anything before his love" (Benedict, *Rule 4: Nihil amori Christi praeponere*). This is the *ileitmotiv* of the whole pontificate of Pope Benedict, and at the same time the only true rule of the Christian in any age.

Edmondo Caruana, O. Carm.

Thoughts On Paul

1. In the beginning

I give thanks to God who, at the beginning of my ministry as Successor of Peter, has granted me to pause in prayer at the Apostle Paul's tomb. It is a deeply-desired pilgrimage, an act of faith that I am making not only in my own name but also in the name of the beloved Diocese of Rome, of which the Lord has constituted me Bishop and Pastor, and of the universal Church, entrusted to my pastoral care. It is a pilgrimage, so to speak, to the roots of mission, the mission that the Risen Christ entrusted to Peter, to the Apostles and in a special way also to Paul, urging him to proclaim the Gospel to the Gentiles, so that he came as far as this city where, after preaching the Kingdom of God for some time (cf. *Ac* 28:31), he poured out his blood, bearing the extreme witness to his Lord who had "grasped" him (*Ph* 3:12) and sent him forth. *Homily*, 25.4.05

APOSTOLIC VOCATION

Apostle to the Gentiles

2. On the road to Damascus

The Lord's call to Paul on the road to Damascus brought him to this: to making Christ the centre of his life, leaving all things for the sublimity of knowing him and the mystery of his love, and subsequently, striving to proclaim him to all, especially the pagans, "that we may spread his name" (*Rm* 1:5). *Homily*, 25.4.05

3. Bearing Christ

On the road to Damascus, Christ's radiant face and strong voice had snatched him from his violent zeal as a persecutor and had kindled within him the new zeal of the Crucified One, who reconciles in his Cross those who are near and far (cf. *Ep* 2:11-22). Paul realized that in Christ the whole of the law is fulfilled and that those who adhere to Christ are united with him and fulfil the law. Bringing Christ, and with Christ the one God, to all peoples became his mission. *Homily*, 17.6.07

4. To evangelize

St Paul traveled tirelessly, taking the Gospel with him. He even felt under a sort of "compulsion" to proclaim the Gospel (cf. 1 *Co* 9:16) - not so much out of concern for the salvation of the single non-baptized person who had not yet been reached by the Gospel, but rather because he was aware that history as a whole could not attain fulfillment until the Gospel had reached the full number (*pléroma*) of Gentiles (cf. *Rm* 11:25). *Speech*, 21.12.07

5. God of all

[A] Fundamental lesson offered by Paul is the universal breadth that characterizes his apostolate. Acutely feeling the problem of the Gentiles, of the pagans, to know God, who in Jesus Christ Crucified and Risen offers salvation to all without exception, he dedicates himself to make this Gospel - literally, "good news" - known, to announce the grace destined to reconcile men with God, self and others. From the first moment he understood that this is a reality that did not concern only the Jews or a certain group of men, but one that had a universal value and concerned everyone, because God is the God of everyone. *Catechesis*, 25.10.06

6. Paul's preaching

After his encounter with the Risen Christ on the road to Damascus, [Paul]... took up the Christological interpretation of the Old Testament made by the First Martyr, deepening and completing it, and consequently became the "Apostle to the Gentiles". The Law is fulfilled, he taught, in the Cross of Christ. And faith in Christ, communion with Christ's love, is the true fulfillment of all the Law. This is the content of Paul's preaching. He showed in this way that the God of Abraham had become the God of all. And all believers in Jesus Christ, as children of Abraham, shared in the promises. *Catechesis*, 10.1.07

7. Catholicity

Strangers have become friends; crossing every border, we recognize one another as brothers and sisters. This brings to fulfilment the mission of St Paul, who knew that he was the "minister of Christ Jesus among the Gentiles... offered up as a pleasing sacrifice, consecrated by the Holy Spirit" (*Rm* 15:16). The purpose of the mission is that humanity itself becomes a living glorification of God, the true worship that God expects: this is the deepest meaning of *catholicity* - a *catholicity* that has already been given to us, towards which we must constantly start out again. *Homily*, 28.6.05

8. Before death

"I for my part am already being poured out like a libation", he writes to the Apostle Timothy. "The time of my dissolution is near. I have fought the good fight, I have finished the race, I have kept the faith" (2 *Tm* 4:6-7). Paul, in prison in Rome, saw death approaching and sketched an evaluation full of recognition and hope. He was at peace with God and with himself and faced death serenely, in the knowledge that he had spent his whole life, sparing no effort, at the service of the Gospel.
Angelus, 28.10.07

9. Paul's example

Today too Christ needs apostles ready to sacrifice themselves. He needs witnesses and martyrs like St Paul. Paul, a former violent persecutor of Christians, when he fell to the ground dazzled by the divine light on the road to Damascus, did not hesitate to change sides to the Crucified One and followed him without second thoughts. He lived and worked for Christ, for him he suffered and died. How timely his example is today!
Homily, 28.6.07

By Grace

10. Election of believers

In the beginning [Saint Paul says] "before the creation of the world" (*Ep* 1:4), in the eternity of God, divine grace is available to enter into action. I am moved by meditating upon this truth: from all eternity we are before the eyes of God and he has decided to save us. *I Salmi dei Vespri*, LEV, 2006, p. 297

11. The calling

[Paul] will explicitly define himself as "apostle by vocation" (cf. *Rm* 1:1; 1 *Co* 1:1) or "apostle by the will of God" (2 *Co* 1:1; *Ep* 1:1; *Col* 1:1), as if to emphasize that his conversion was not the result of a development of thought or reflection, but the fruit of divine intervention, an unforeseeable, divine grace. *Catechesis*, 25.10.06

12. By grace

Divine charity is the strength that transforms the life of Saul of Tarsus and makes him the Apostle to the Gentiles. Writing to the Christians at Corinth, St Paul confesses that God's grace worked the extraordinary event of conversion in him: "By the grace of God I am what I am, and his grace toward me was not in vain" (1 *Co* 15:10). On the one hand, he feels the weight of having hindered the spread of Christ's message; but on the other, he lives in the joy of having met the Risen Lord and having been enlightened and transformed by his light. *Homily*, 25.1.06

13. Strength from grace

"I worked harder than any of them, though it was not I, but the grace of God which is with me" (1 *Co* 15: 10). Tirelessly, as though the work of the mission depended entirely upon his own efforts, St Paul was nevertheless always motivated by the profound conviction that all his energy came from God's grace at work in him. *Homily*, 25.1.08

14. Apostle by vocation

Paul knew he was "called to be an apostle", that is, that he had not presented himself as a candidate, nor was his a human appointment, but solely by a divine call and election.

The Apostle to the Gentiles repeats several times in his Letters that his whole life is a fruit of God's freely given and merciful grace (cf. 1 *Co* 15:9-10; 2 *Co* 4:1; *Ga* 1:15). He was chosen to proclaim "the Gospel of God" (*Rm* 1:1), to disseminate the announcement of divine Grace which in Christ reconciles man with God, himself and others. *Homily*, 18.6.07

15. Grace of Christ

The Apostle wishes [the Ephesians] "grace and peace from God our Father and the Lord Jesus Christ" (*Ep* 1:2). Grace is the power that transforms man and the world; peace is the mature fruit of this transformation. Christ is grace; Christ is peace.
Homily, 29.11.06

ENCOUNTER WITH JESUS

Christ: the face of God

16. Grandeur of revelation

God did not only speak, but loved us very realistically; he loved us to the point of the death of his own Son. It is precisely here that we are shown the full grandeur of revelation that has, as it were, inflicted the wounds in the heart of God himself. Then each one of us can say personally, together with St Paul, I live "a life of faith in the Son of God, who loved me and gave himself for me" (*Ga* 2:20).

Let us pray to the Lord that the truth of these words may be deeply impressed in our hearts, together with his joy and with his responsibility. *Homily*, 29.6.05

17. To know God

The subject "God" is essential. St Paul says in his Letter to the Ephesians: "Remember that you were at that time... having no hope and without God.... But now in Christ Jesus you who once were far off have been brought near" (*Ep* 2:12-13). Thus, life has a meaning that guides me even through difficulties.

It is therefore necessary to return to God the Creator, to the God who is creative reason, and then to find Christ, who is the living Face of God. *Speech*, 22.2.07

18. Profession of faith

In a passage of his First Letter to the Corinthians: "Although there may be so-called gods in heaven or on earth for us there is only "one God, the Father, from whom are all things and for whom we exist, and one Lord, Jesus Christ, through whom are all things and through whom we exist" (1 *Co* 8:5-6). Thus, from the outset the disciples recognized the Risen Jesus as the One who is our brother in humanity but is also one with God; the One who, with his coming into the world and throughout his life, in his death and in his Resurrection, brought us God and in a new and unique way made God present in the world: the One, therefore, who gives meaning and hope to our life; in fact, it is in him that we encounter the true Face of God that we find what we really need in order to live. *Speech*, 11.6.07

19. Hope and glory

"May he [God] truly enlighten the eyes of your mind, so that you may understand what hope you have been called to, what treasure of glory his inheritance among the saints entails" (*Ep* 1:18). This is the wish Paul raises to the God of our Lord Jesus Christ, the Father of glory… We shall never thank God our Father enough for this immense treasure of hope and glory, given to us as a gift in his Son Jesus. Our constant effort is to let ourselves be continually enlightened by him, in order to know ever more deeply this mysterious gift. *Speech*, 28.5.05

Centrality of Christ

20. Lesson
The existence [of Paul is] that of an Apostle who wants to "become all things to all men" (1 *Co* 9:22) without reserve. From here we draw a very important lesson: what counts is to place Jesus Christ at the centre of our lives, so that our identity is marked essentially by the encounter, by communion with Christ and with his Word. *Catechesis*, 25.10.06

21. Project
The Apostle to the Gentiles [reminds] us that if we die with Christ, "we shall also live with him; if we endure, we shall also reign with him; if we deny him, he also will deny us" (2 *Tm* 2:11-12). The entire plan of life of the Christian can only be modelled on Christ, all of it with him, for him and in him, to the glory of God the Father. *Homily*, 14.12.07

22. Giving oneself
"The life I now live in the flesh I live by faith in the Son of God, who loved me and gave himself for me" (*Ga* 2:20).

Paul, therefore, no longer lives for himself, for his own justice. He lives for Christ and with Christ: in giving of himself, he is no longer seeking and building himself up. This is the new justice, the new orientation given to us by the Lord, given to us by faith.

Before the Cross of Christ, the extreme expression of his self-giving, there is no one who can boast of himself, of his own self-made justice, made for himself! *Catechesis*, 8.11.06

23. Christian identity

Christian identity is composed of precisely two elements: this restraint from seeking oneself by oneself but instead receiving oneself from Christ and giving oneself with Christ, thereby participating personally in the life of Christ himself to the point of identifying with him and sharing both his death and his life. This is what Paul wrote in his *Letter to the Romans*: "[A]ll of us... were baptized into his death... we were buried therefore with him... we have been united with him.... So you also must consider yourselves dead to sin and alive to God in Christ Jesus" (*Rm* 6:3, 4, 5, 11). *Catechesis*, 8.11.06

24. Mystical union

Although faith unites us closely to Christ, it emphasizes the distinction between us and him; but according to Paul, Christian life also has an element that we might describe as "mystical", since it entails an identification of ourselves with Christ and of Christ with us. *Catechesis*, 8.11.06

25. Conquered

Paul was utterly "conquered" by Christ - *"comprehensus sum a Christo Iesu"* (cf. *Ph* 3:12) - and like Paul he can exhort the elders with full authority because it is no longer he who lives, but Christ lives in him - *"vivo autem iam non ego, vivit vero in me Christus"* (*Ga* 2:20). *Homily*, 24.3.06

26. Transformation of self

You have become one in Christ (cf. *Ga* 3:28). Not just one thing, but one, one only, one single new subject. This liberation of our "I" from its isolation, this finding oneself in a new subject means finding oneself within the vastness of God and being drawn into a life which has now moved out of the context of "dying and becoming". *Homily*, 15.4.06

27. Discipleship

St Paul... assures the Christians of Corinth: "You are in our hearts, to die together and to live together" (2 *Co* 7:3). What takes place between the Apostle and his Christians must obviously apply first of all to the relationship between Christians and Jesus himself: dying together, living together, being in his Heart as he is in ours. *Catechesis*, 27.9.06

Mystery of the Cross

28. Scandal of the cross

The Mosaic Law was totally fulfilled in Jesus, who revealed God's wisdom and love through the mystery of the Cross, "a stumbling block to Jews and an absurdity to Gentiles; but to those who are called, Jews and Greeks alike, Christ is the power of God and the wisdom of God" (1 Co 1:23-24). *Homily*, 19.3.06

29. Cross of Christ

The Apostle Paul says: "We preach Christ crucified, a stumbling block to Jews and folly to Gentiles" (1 Co 1:23). Christians, however, do not exalt just any cross but the Cross which Jesus sanctified with his sacrifice, the fruit and testimony of immense love. *Angelus*, 17.9.06

30. Scientia Crucis

The Apostle can affirm that he wants nothing except "Jesus Christ and him crucified" (1 Co 2:2). It is true: the Cross shows "the breadth and length and height and depth" - the cosmic dimensions is the meaning - of a love that surpasses all knowledge, a love that goes beyond what is known and fills us "with all the fullness of God" (*Ep* 3:18-19). *Catechesis*, 12.4.06

31. Sign of love

The manifestation of divine love is total and perfect in the Cross where, we are told by Saint Paul, "God proves his love for us in that while we still were sinners Christ died for us" (*Rm* 5:8). Therefore, each one of us can truly say: "Christ loved me and gave himself up for me" (cf *Ep* 5:2). Redeemed by his blood, no human life is useless or of little value, because each of us is loved personally by Him with a passionate and faithful love, a love without limits.
Message, 27.1.07

32. Christ our peace

It strikes us... the beauty of the vision illustrate by the apostle Paul (*Ep* 2:13-18): Christ is our peace. He has reconciled all, Jews and pagans, by uniting them in his body. He has overcome in his body the opposition and has united us all in his peace.
Speech, 25.7.06

Way of the Cross

33. Christ as example

In a famous passage from his Letter to the Philippians, the Apostle Paul says that Christ "emptied himself, taking the form of a servant" (2:7). He, Christ, is the example at which to look. In the Gospel, he told his disciples he had come "not to be served but to serve" (cf. *Mt* 20:28). *Speech*, 18.2.06

34. Kenosis

Saint Paul says to all, especially of course to those who work in God's field: "have in yourselves the mind of Christ Jesus". His mind was such that, faced with the destiny of humanity, he could hardly bear to remain in glory, but had to stoop down and do the incredible, take upon himself the utter poverty of a human life even to the point of suffering on the Cross. This is the mind of Jesus Christ: feeling impelled to bring to humanity the light of the Father, to help us by forming the Kingdom of God with us and in us. *Speech*, 14.9.06

35. For others

Referring to Paul's words to the Corinthians, "the love of Christ urges us on" (2 *Co* 5:14), I stressed that "the consciousness that, in Christ, God has given himself for us, even unto death, must inspire us to live no longer for ourselves but for him, and, with him, for others" (*Deus caritas est*, 33). *Homily*, 1.3.06

36. Stigmata

In the dispute on the right way of seeing and living the Gospel, it is not, in the end, the arguments that decide our thought: it is the reality of life that decides, communion lived and suffered with Jesus, not only in ideas or words but in the depths of our existence, also involving the body, the flesh. The bruises that the Apostle received in the long history of his passion are the witness of the presence of the Cross of Jesus in St Paul's body; they are his stigmata. Thus, one can say that it is not circumcision that saves: these stigmata are the consequence of his Baptism, the expression of his dying with Jesus, day after day, the sure sign of his being a new creature (cf. *Ga* 6:15). *Homily*, 17.6.07

The Risen One

37. Joy of Easter

God's love for us, which began with creation, became visible in the mystery of the Cross, in that kenosis of God, in that self-emptying, that abasement of the Son of God which we heard proclaimed by the Apostle Paul... in the magnificent hymn to Christ in the Letter to the Philippians. Yes, the Cross reveals the fullness of God's love for us. It is a crucified love which does not stop at the scandal of Good Friday but culminates in the joy of the Resurrection. *Homily*, 29.3.07

38. Victory over evil

Evil in all its forms does not have the last word. The final triumph, the triumph of truth and love, is Christ's! If we are willing to suffer and die with him, St Paul will remind us... his life will become our life (cf. *Rm* 6:9). Our Christian life is supported by and built upon this certainty. *Catechesis*, 4.4.07

39. Event of the resurrection

The Resurrection of Christ is central to Christianity. It is a fundamental truth to be reasserted vigorously in every epoch, since to deny it, as has been, and continues to be attempted, or to transform it into a purely spiritual event, is to thwart our very faith. St Paul states: "If Christ has not been raised, then our preaching is in vain and your faith is in vain" (1 *Co* 15:14). *Regina Caeli*, 30.4.06

40. Commission

In St Paul's First Letter to the Corinthians, we find the oldest account we have of the Resurrection. Paul faithfully received it from the witnesses. This account first speaks of Christ's death for our sins, of his burial and of his Resurrection which took place the third day, and then says: "[Christ] was seen by Cephas, then by the Twelve..." (1 *Co* 15:4). Thus, the importance of the mandate conferred upon Peter to the end of time is summed up: being a witness of the Risen Christ. *Homily*, 7.5.05

41. Witnesses of the Risen One

"If, then, you have been raised with Christ", St Paul exhorts us, "seek the things that are above.... Set your minds on things that are above, not on things that are on earth" (*Col* 3:1-2). This does not mean cutting oneself off from one's daily commitments, neglecting earthly realities; rather, it means reviving every human activity with a supernatural breath, it means making ourselves joyful proclaimers and witnesses of the Resurrection of Christ, living for eternity (cf. *Jn* 20:25; *Lk* 24:33-34). *Catechesis*, 19.4.06

42. Lamb of God

The Cross, - for the world a folly, for many believers a scandal-, is in fact the "wisdom of God" for those who allow themselves to be touched right to the innermost depths of their being, *"for God's foolishness is wiser than human wisdom, and God's weakness is stronger than human strength"* (1 Co 1:25). Moreover, the Crucifix, which after the Resurrection would carry forever the marks of his passion, exposes the "distortions" and lies about God that underlie violence, vengeance and exclusion. Christ is the Lamb of God who takes upon himself the sins of the world and eradicates hatred from the heart of humankind. This is the true "revolution" that He brings about: love. *Message*, 27.1.07

Life in the Spirit

Action of the Spirit

43. Unity

The Holy Spirit gives understanding.
Overcoming the "breach" begun in Babel - the confusion of hearts, putting us one against the other - the Spirit opens borders. The People of God who found its first configuration on Mt Sinai, now becomes enlarged to the point of recognizing no limitations... St Paul explains and underlines this in the Second Reading when he says: "It was in one Spirit that all of us, whether Jew or Greek, slave or free, were baptized into one body. All of us have been given to drink of the one Spirit" (1 *Co* 12:13). *Homily*, 15.5.05

44. Beatitude

We are indeed blessed when the Holy Spirit opens us to the joy of believing and makes us enter the great family of Christians, his Church. For all her rich diversity, in the variety of gifts, ministries and works, the Church is already one, since "it is the same God who inspires them all in every one" (1 *Co* 12:4). *Homily*, 1.12.06

45. Profession of faith

As Saint Paul [reminds] us (1 *Co* 12:3), the Spirit is the enduring source of our faith and unity. He awakens within us true knowledge of Jesus and he puts on our lips the words of faith that enable us to acknowledge the Lord. *Homily*, 1.12.06

46. Life in communion

"The grace of the Lord Jesus Christ and the love of God and the fellowship of the Holy Spirit be with you all" (2 *Co* 13:14). These words, probably echoed in the worship of the newborn Church, emphasize how the free gift of the Father in Jesus Christ is realized and expressed in the communion brought about by the Holy Spirit... Communion is a gift with very real consequences. It lifts us from our loneliness, from being closed in on ourselves, and makes us sharers in the love that unites us to God and to one another. *Catechesis*, 29.3.06

47. The Consoler

In the second letter to the Corinthians Saint Paul affirms with conviction that "The God of all consolation... consoles us in our every tribulation, so that also we may console those who find themselves in any kind of affliction" (1,3-4). We know well that the consolation promised by the Holy Spirit is not made up of merely good words; instead it translates

into an enlargement of the mind and heart. This allows one to see one's own situation within the greater picture of the whole of creation that is suffering the pangs of giving birth while waiting of the revelation of the children of God (Cf. *Rm* 8:19-25).
Message, 25.12.06

The Spirit within our Hearts

48. Indwelling of the Spirit

Paul's reflection on the Spirit... not only explained his influence on the action of Christians, but also on their being. Indeed, it is he who said that the Spirit of God dwells in us (cf. *Rm* 8:9; 1 *Co* 3:16) and that "God has sent the Spirit of his Son into our hearts" (*Ga* 4:6). *Catechesis*, 15.11.06

49. Spirit of Jesus

St Paul spoke directly of the "Spirit of Christ" (*Rm* 8:9), of the "Spirit of his Son" (cf. *Ga* 4:6) or of the "Spirit of Jesus Christ" (*Ph* 1:19). It is as though he wanted to say that not only is God the Father visible in the Son (cf. *Jn* 14:9), but that the Spirit of God also expresses himself in the life and action of the Crucified and Risen Lord! *Catechesis*, 15.11.06

50. Prayer and the Spirit

Paul teaches us another important thing: he says that there is no true prayer without the presence of the Spirit within us. He wrote: "The Spirit helps us in our weakness; for we do not know how to pray as we ought, but the Spirit himself intercedes for us with sighs too deep for words. And he who searches the hearts of men knows what is the mind of the Spirit, because the Spirit intercedes for the saints according to the will of God" (*Rm* 8:26-27)... It is an invitation to be increasingly sensitive, more attentive to this presence of the Spirit in us, to transform it into prayer, to feel this presence and thus to learn to pray, to speak to the Father as children in the Holy Spirit. *Catechesis*, 15.11.06

51. To live by the Spirit
"To each is given the manifestation of the Spirit for the common good" [1 *Co* 12:7]. To manifest the Spirit, to live by the Spirit, is not to live for oneself alone, but to let oneself be conformed to Christ Jesus by becoming, like him, the servant of his brothers and sisters. *Homily*, 1.12.06

52. Inheritance
According to St Paul, the Spirit is a generous downpayment given to us by God himself as a deposit and at the same time, a guarantee of our future inheritance (cf. 2 *Co* 1:22; 5:5; *Ep* 1:13-14). *Catechesis*, 15.11.06

Adopted Children

53. Divine adoption

The Apostle Paul writes: "Blessed be the God and Father of our Lord Jesus Christ ... even as he chose us in him before the foundation of the world ... He destined us in love to be his sons through Jesus Christ" (*Ep* 1:3-5). Before the creation of the world, before our coming into existence, the heavenly Father chose us personally, calling us to enter into a filial relationship with Him, through Jesus, the Incarnate Word, under the guidance of the Holy Spirit. *Message*, 5.3.06

54. Sons of God thanks to the Spirit

"You did not receive the spirit of slavery to fall back into fear, but you have received the spirit of sonship through which we cry, 'Abba! Father!'"(*Rm* 8:2, 15). As children, we can call God "Father"... This is our greatest dignity: to be not merely images but also children of God. And it is an invitation to live our sonship, to be increasingly aware that we are adoptive sons in God's great family. *Catechesis*, 15.11.06

55. Filial responsibility

The Holy Spirit [says Saint Paul] makes us sons and daughters of God. He involves us in the same responsibility that God has for his world, for the whole of humanity. He teaches us to look at the world, others and ourselves with God's eyes. We do not do good as slaves who are not free to act otherwise, but we do it because we are personally responsible for the world; because we love truth and goodness, because we love God himself and therefore, also his creatures. This is the true freedom to which the Holy Spirit wants to lead us.
Homily, 3.6.06

Theme of Freedom

56. Freedom of the children of God

We want the true, great freedom, the freedom of heirs, the freedom of children of God. In this world, so full of fictitious forms of freedom that destroy the environment and the human being, let us learn true freedom by the power of the Holy Spirit; to build the school of freedom; to show others by our lives that we are free and how beautiful it is to be truly free with the true freedom of God's children. *Homily*, 3.6.06

57. Freedom from sin

"God sent forth his Son... to redeem those who were under the law, so that we might receive adoption as sons" (*Ga* 4:4-5). The Incarnate Word transforms human life from within, sharing with us his being as Son of the Father. He became like us in order for us to become like him: children of the Son, hence, people free from the law of sin. *Homily*, 31.12.07

58. Freedom as a service

[Paul says in the] letter to the Galatians: "You were called to freedom, brethren; only do not use your freedom as an opportunity for the flesh, but through love be servants of one another" (5:13). Freedom is mutual service. *Speech*, 28.11.06

CHRISTIAN EXPERIENCE

59. Definition
[Paul addresses] all who are distinguished in the world by the fact that they "call on the name of Our Lord Jesus Christ" (1 *Co* 1:2). This is our definition: we belong among those who call on the Name of the Lord Jesus Christ. *Catechesis*, 22.11.06

In the Heart of Jesus

60. Right path
I want to underline this admonition of St Paul: "Have this mind among yourselves, which was in Christ Jesus". To learn to feel as Jesus felt; to conform our way of thinking, deciding and acting to the sentiments of Jesus. We will take up this path if we look to conform our sentiments to those of Jesus. Let us take up the right path. *Catechesis*, 26.10.05

61. Familiarity
In Paul's Letter to the Ephesians, one would read that what is important is to "learn Christ" (4:20): therefore, not only and not so much to listen to his teachings and words as rather to know him in person, that is, his humanity and his divinity, his mystery and his beauty. In fact, he is not only a Teacher but a Friend,

indeed, a Brother. How will we be able to get to know him properly by being distant? Closeness, familiarity and habit make us discover the true identity of Jesus Christ. *Catechesis*, 6.9.06

62. Friendship with Jesus

Friendship means sharing in thought and will. We must put into practice this communion of thought with Jesus, as St Paul tells us in his Letter to the Philippians (cf. 2:2-5). And this communion of thought is not a purely intellectual thing, but a sharing of sentiments and will, hence, also of actions. This means that we should know Jesus in an increasingly personal way, listening to him, living together with him, staying with him. *Homily*, 13.4.06

63. Thinking with the heart

St Paul cries to us in God's Name: "Your attitude must be Christ's - *Touto phroneite en hymin ho kai en Christo Iesou*". Learn to think as Christ thought, learn to think with him! And this thinking is not only the thinking of the mind, but also a thinking of the heart. *Homily*, 7.11.06

64. True progress

"in him all things were created, in heaven and on earth, visible and invisible... and in him all things hold together" (cf. vv. 16-17)... In other words, St

Paul tells us: yes, there is progress in history. There is, we could say, an evolution of history. Progress is all that which brings us closer to Christ and thus closer to a united humanity, to true humanism. *Catechesis*, 4.1.06

65. A new spirit
The new spirit [is that] of those who have found the meaning of life in Jesus and in his Paschal Mystery and realize that henceforth everything must refer to him. This was the attitude of the Apostle Paul who affirmed that he had left everything behind in order to know Christ (*Ph* 3:10-11). *Angelus*, 26.2.06

Fruits of the Spirit

66. Love
It is not without significance that when Paul lists the various elements that constitute the fruit of the Spirit he puts love first: "the fruit of the Spirit is love, joy, peace", etc. (*Ga* 5:22)... The Spirit stimulates us to weave charitable relations with all people. Therefore, when we love we make room for the Spirit and give him leeway to express himself fully within us. *Catechesis*, 15.11.06

67. Harmony
The Apostle, aware of how easy it is to succumb to the ever latent threat of conflicts and disputes, urged the young Community at Philippi to concord and unity. To the Galatians he was to indicate forcefully that the whole law finds its fullness in the one precept of love; and he exhorts them to proceed in accordance with the Spirit so as to avoid acts of the flesh - discord, jealousy, disagreement, division, factions, envy - and thus to obtain instead the fruit of the Spirit which is love (cf. *Ga* 5:14-23). *Speech*, 30.5.05

68. Fraternal admonishment
[Paul writes:] "encourage one another...". Fraternal correction is a work of mercy. None of us sees

himself or his shortcomings clearly. It is therefore an act of love to complement one another, to help one another see each other better, and correct each other. *Speech*, 3.10.05

69. Generosity

It is wisdom and virtue not to set one's heart on the goods of this world for all things are transient, all things can suddenly end. For us Christians, the real treasure that we must ceaselessly seek consists in the "things above... where Christ is seated at God's right hand"; St Paul reminds us (*Col* 3:1-3). *Angelus*, 5.8.07

70. Joy

"Always rejoice in the Lord. I repeat, rejoice, the Lord is close" (*Ph* 4:4.5). Here we understand the reason why Paul, in all his sufferings, in all his trials, could only tell others to "rejoice"; he could say this because joy was present within him... If the loved one, the love, the greatest gift of my life, is close to me; if I can be convinced that the person who loves me is beside me even in troubling situations, in the depths of my heart dwells a joy that is greater than all suffering. The Apostle could say "be happy" because the Lord is close to each one of us. *Angelus*, 3.10.05

71. Perseverance

Perseverance in good, even if it is misunderstood and opposed, always reaches a landing place of light, fruitfulness and peace. This is what St Paul reminded the Galatians: "If [a man] sows in the field of the flesh, he will reap a harvest of corruption; but if his seed-ground is the spirit, he will reap everlasting life. Let us not grow weary of doing good; if we do not relax our efforts, in due time we shall reap our harvest" (*Ga* 6:8-9). *Cetechesis*, 17.8.05

72. Interior peace

[Saint Paul says: "Live in peace", (2 *Co* 13:11)]... Only if we are grounded in deep inner peace can we also be men and women of peace in the world and for others. *Speech*, 3.10.05

73. Kingdom of God

We find one of the most beautiful definitions of the Kingdom of God in the Second Reading. It is a text that belongs to the exhortational part of the Letter to the Romans. The Apostle Paul, after urging Christians always to allow themselves to be guided by love and not to be objects of scandal for those who are weak in faith, recalls that the Kingdom of God is "righteousness and peace and joy in the Holy Spirit" (*Rm* 14:17). *Homily*, 6.5.06

Faith, Hope and Love

Faith

74. Believing

God [as Paul writes] has given us a spirit of wisdom and "the eyes of our mind in order to understand what hope he has called us to, what treasure of glory his inheritance among the saints holds, and the extraordinary greatness of his power towards us believers, according to the efficacy of his strength, that he manifested in Christ" (Cf. *Ep* 1:17-20). Believing means to abandon oneself to God, and to entrust him with our fate. Believing is to establish a deeply personal bond with our creator and redeemer through the Holy Spirit, making it so that this bond is the foundation of a whole life. *Speech*, 28.5.06

75. In the hands of the Lord

We must be sure that however burdensome and tempestuous the trials that await us may be, we will never be left on our own, we will never fall out of the Lord's hands, those hands that created us and now sustain us on our journey through life. As St Paul was to confess: "he who has begun the good work in you will carry it through to completion" (*Ph* 1:6). *Catechesis*, 7.12.05

76. Optimism

The Good Shepherd, acts in souls with his grace. "My grace is sufficient for you" (2 *Co* 12:9), the Apostle Paul heard the Lord answer when he asked the Lord to spare him suffering. May this very awareness always nourish your faith and stimulate within you the search for ways to reach the hearts of all with the healthy optimism that you must always spread around you. *Speech*, 21.9.06

77. Trust

Even in the darkest moments of our lives, we know that God is never absent. Saint Paul reminds us that "in everything God works for good with those who love him" (*Rm* 8:28). *Speech*, 7.5.07

Hope

78. Receiving hope

Paul reminds the Ephesians that before their encounter with Christ they were "without hope and without God in the world" (*Ep* 2:12)… To come to know God—the true God—means to receive hope. *Spe Salvi*, 3

79. Christian hope

[Paul] says to the Thessalonians: you must not "grieve as others do who have no hope" (1 *Th* 4:13). Here too we see as a distinguishing mark of Christians the fact that they have a future: it is not that they know the details of what awaits them, but they know in general terms that their life will not end in emptiness. Only when the future is certain as a positive reality does it become possible to live the present as well. *Spe Salvi*, 2

80. To build up hope
We need to build up hope, weaving the fabric of a society that, by relaxing its grip on the threads of life, is losing the true sense of hope. This loss, according to Saint Paul, is the self-imposed curse of "heartless persons" (cf. *Rm* 1:31). *Speech* (1), 12.5.07

81. Roots
The hope of Christians is turned to the future but remains firmly rooted in an event of the past. In the fullness of time, the Son of God was born of the Virgin Mary: "Born of a woman, born under the law", as the Apostle Paul writes (*Ga* 4:4). *Angelus*, 27.11.05

Charity

82. Proclamation
For Christians, the words of St Paul are valid: "The love of Christ impels us" (2 *Co* 5:14). The charity that moved the Father to send his Son into the world, and moved the Son to offer himself for us even to death on the Cross, that same charity has been poured out by the Holy Spirit in the hearts of believers. Every

baptized person, as a vine united to the branch, can therefore cooperate in the mission of Jesus, which can be summarized thus: to bring to every person the good news that "God is love" and, precisely for this reason, wants to save the world. *Angelus*, 22.10.06

83. Giving oneself

Saint Paul, in his hymn to charity (cf. 1 *Co* 13), teaches us that it is always more than activity alone: "If I give away all I have, and if I deliver my body to be burned, but do not have love, I gain nothing" (v. 3). This hymn must be the Magna Carta of all ecclesial service... Practical activity will always be insufficient, unless it visibly expresses a love for man, a love nourished by an encounter with Christ. My deep personal sharing in the needs and sufferings of others becomes a sharing of my very self with them: if my gift is not to prove a source of humiliation, I must give to others not only something that is my own, but my very self; I must be personally present in my gift. *Deus caritas est*, 34

84. Deus caritas est

Humanity today stands in need of this essential message, incarnate in Jesus Christ: God is love. Everything must start from here and everything must lead to here, every pastoral action, every theological treatise. As St Paul said, "If I... have not love I gain nothing" (cf. 1 *Co* 13:3). All charisms lose their meaning and value without love, thanks to which instead, all compete to build the Mystical Body of Christ. *Homily* (2), 22.4.07

85. Unconditional love

The human being needs unconditional love. He needs the certainty which makes him say: "neither death, nor life, nor angels, nor principalities, nor things present, nor things to come, nor powers, nor height, nor depth, nor anything else in all creation, will be able to separate us from the love of God in Christ Jesus our Lord" (*Rm* 8:38-39). If this absolute love exists, with its absolute certainty, then—only then—is man "redeemed", whatever should happen to him in his particular circumstances. *Spe salvi*, 26

86. Justice and charity

Justice by itself is not enough to form truly human relations of brotherhood within society... [As Paul proclaims: "Charity is patient, charity is benevolent" (1 *Co* 13,4)]. In a word, charity not only allows justice to become more creative and to tackle new challenges, it also inspires and purifies the efforts of humanity that try to reach authentic justice. In this way a society that is worthy of man can be built. *Message*, 28.4.07

87. Mission of charity

St Paul, the Apostle to the Gentiles, wrote: "The love of Christ impels us" (2 *Co* 5:14). May every Christian make these words his own, in the joyful experience of being a missionary of Love wherever Providence has placed him, with humility and courage, serving his neighbour with no ulterior motives and drawing strength from prayer for a cheerful and industrious charity. *Angelus*, 1.10.06

Works and Faith

88. Faith of a Christian

Paul wrote in his *Letter to the Romans*: "We hold that a man is justified by faith apart from works of law" (3:28)... Paul states with absolute clarity that this condition of life does not depend on our possible good works but on the pure grace of God: "[We] are justified by his grace as a gift, through the redemption which is in Christ Jesus" (*Rm* 3:24). *Catechesis*, 8.11.06

89. Justification

Paul, who claims that we are justified by God not by virtue of our actions but through our faith (cf. *Ga* 2:16; *Rm* 3:28). St Paul is opposed to the pride of man who thinks he does not need the love of God that precedes us; he is opposed to the pride of self-justification without grace, simply given and undeserved. *Catechesis*, 28.6.06

90. Law and grace

The Wisdom of God is contained in the Decalogue. This is why Jesus affirms in the Gospel that to "enter into life" it is necessary to observe the commandments (cf. *Mk* 10:19). It is necessary, but not sufficient! In fact, as St Paul says, salvation does not come from the law, but from Grace. *Homily*, 15.10.06

Conversion

91. Human frailty

In order to respond to the call of God and start on our journey, it is not necessary to be already perfect. Weaknesses and human limitations do not present an obstacle, as long as they help make us more aware of the fact that we are in need of the redeeming grace of Christ. This is the experience of St Paul who confessed: "I will all the more gladly boast of my weaknesses, that the power of Christ may rest upon me" (2 *Co* 12:9). To "boast of my weaknesses" is to accept goodheartedly and willingly one's own situation of frailty: the limits of one's strength, suffering,, being conscious of the Lord's closeness, trusting in his power, despite our weaknesses.
Message, 5.3.06

92. The way

St Paul's words to the Thessalonians are brought to completion in us: "You turned to God from idols, to serve him who is the living and true God" (1 *Th* 1:9). This conversion is the beginning of the walk of holiness that the Christian is called to achieve in his own life. The saint is the person who is so fascinated by the beauty of God and by his perfect truth as to be progressively transformed by it. Because of this beauty and truth, he is ready to renounce everything, even himself. Love of God is enough for him, experienced in humble and disinterested service to one's neighbour, especially towards those who cannot give back in return. *Homily*, 23.10.05

Sanctification

93. Communion with Christ

Saint Paul reminds us that through Christ we are no longer strangers and aliens but citizens with the saints and members of the household of God, growing into a holy temple, a dwelling place for God (cf. *Ep* 2:19-22). This sublime portrayal of a life of communion engages all aspects of our lives as Christians. *Speech*, 17.3.06

94. "Aim for perfection" (2 *Cor* 13:11)

These words [of Paul] invite us to be what we are: images of God, beings created in relation to the Lord, "mirrors" where the Lord's light is reflected. Not to live Christianity according to the letter, not to understand Sacred Scripture according to the letter is often difficult, historically disputable; but we must go beyond the letter, our present reality, towards the Lord who speaks to us and hence, to union with God. *Speech*, 3.10.05

95. Universal holiness

In his First Letter to the Corinthians, St Paul addresses "those sanctified in Christ Jesus, called to be saints together with all those who in every place call on the name of our Lord Jesus Christ" (1 *Co* 1:2).

Indeed, Christians are already saints because Baptism unites them to Jesus and to his Paschal Mystery, but at the same time they must become so by conforming themselves every more closely to him. *Angelus*, 1.11.07

96. Vocation
Paul reminds us that all men are called to become holy and immaculate in love (cf. *Ep* 1:4), in the image of our Creator. *Angelus*, 8.12.05

97. Holiness
To become saints means to completely fulfill what we already are, raised to the dignity of God's adopted children, in Christ Jesus (cf. *Ep* 1:5; *Rm* 8:14-17). *Angelus*, 1.11.05

CHURCH OF GOD

98. Charity is the heart of the Church
My venerable predecessor Pope John Paul II, stated that "many things are necessary for the Church's journey through history, not least in this new century; but without charity (*agape*) all will be in vain. It is again the Apostle Paul who in his *hymn to love* reminds us: even if we speak the tongues of men and of angels, and if we have faith 'to move mountains', but are without love, all will come to 'nothing' (cf. 1 *Co* 13:2). Love is truly the 'heart' of the Church". *Letter*, 27.5.07

People of God, body of Christ, temple of God

99. Sign of unity

Paul knows that he has been sent to proclaim a "mystery", a divine plan that only in the fullness of time has been carried out and revealed in Christ: namely, that "the Gentiles have become fellow heirs, members of the same body, and sharers in the promise in Christ Jesus through the Gospel" (*Ep* 3:6). This *mystery* is accomplished, in salvation history, *in the Church*, the new People in which, now that the old dividing wall has been broken down, Jews and pagans find themselves united. Like Christ himself, the Church is not only the *instrument* of unity, but also its *efficacious* sign. Homily, 29.11.06

100. Centrality of the Church

For Paul, adherence to the Church was brought about by a direct intervention of Christ, who in revealing himself on the road to Damascus identified himself with the Church and made Paul realize that persecution of the Church was persecution of himself, the Lord. In fact, the Risen One said to Paul, persecutor of the Church: "Saul, Saul, why do you persecute me?" (*Ac* 9:4). In persecuting the Church, he was persecuting

Christ. Paul, therefore, was at the same time converted to Christ and to the Church. This leads one to understand why the Church later became so present in Paul's thoughts, heart and activity. *Catechesis*, 22.11.06

101. Christ and the Church

On the road to Damascus, Saul hears the disturbing question: "Why do you persecute me?". Falling to the ground and interiorly troubled, he asked: "Who are you, Lord?", receiving that answer which is the basis of his conversion: "I am Jesus, whom you are persecuting" (*Ac* 9:4-5). Paul understood in an instant what he would later express in his writings: that the Church forms a single body of which Christ is the Head. And so, from a persecutor of Christians he became the Apostle to the Gentiles. *Homily*, 25.1.06

102. Mystical body

Paul makes us understand that not only does the belonging of the Church to Christ exist, but also a certain form of equality and identification of the Church with Christ himself. From this, therefore, derive the greatness and nobility of the Church, that is, of all of us who are part of her: from our being members of Christ, an extension as it were of his personal presence in the world. *Catechesis*, 22.11.06

103. Charisms of the Christian community
Underlining the need for unity does not mean that ecclesial life should be standardized or levelled out in accordance with a single way of operating. Elsewhere, Paul taught: "Do not quench the Spirit" (1 *Th* 5:19), that is, make room generously for the unforeseeable dynamism of the charismatic manifestations of the Spirit, who is an ever new source of energy and vitality. *Catechesis*, 22.11.06

104. Do not quench charisms
St Paul [exhorts] in his First Letter to the Thessalonians: do not extinguish charisms. If the Lord gives us new gifts we must be grateful, even if at times they may be inconvenient. And it is beautiful that without an initiative of the hierarchy but with an initiative from below, as people say, but which also truly comes from on High, that is, as a gift of the Holy Spirit, new forms of life are being born in the Church just as, moreover, they were born down the ages. *Speech*, 22.2.07

105. Bride of Christ
Then, there is also a Pauline Letter that presents the Church as Christ's Bride (cf. *Ep* 5:21-33). With this, Paul borrowed an ancient prophetic metaphor which made the People of Israel the Bride of the God of the Covenant (cf. *Ho* 2:4, 21; *Is* 54:5-8). He did so to

express the intimacy of the relationship between Christ and his Church, both in the sense that she is the object of the most tender love on the part of her Lord, and also in the sense that love must be mutual and that we too therefore, as members of the Church, must show him passionate faithfulness. *Catechesis*, 22.11.06

106. Holy city

Just as in their love man and woman become "one flesh", so Christ and humanity gathered in the Church become through Christ's love "one spirit" (cf. 1 *Co* 6:17; *Ep* 5:29ff.). Paul calls Christ the new, the last Adam: definitive man. And he calls him "a life-giving spirit" (1 *Co* 15:45). With him, we become one; with him, the Church becomes a life-giving spirit. The holy City, where there is no longer a temple because it is inhabited by God, is the image of this community that is formed from Christ. *Homily*, 10.12.06

107. Spiritual body

Although she is a body, the Church is the Body of Christ, hence, she is a spiritual body, as St Paul said. She is a spiritual reality. I think this is very important: that people see that the Church is not a supranational organization nor an administrative body or power, that she is not a social agency, but indeed that although she does social and supranational work, she is a spiritual body. *Speech*, 22.11.07

108. Family of God
Paul compare[s], in the Letter to the Ephesians, the matrimonial relationship to the spousal communion that happens between Christ and the Church (cf. *Ep* 5:25-33). Even more, we can maintain that the Apostle indirectly models the life of the entire Church on that of the family. And the Church, in reality, is the family of God. *Catechesis*, 7.2.07

109. The Holy Spirit and the Church
St Paul's doctrine reveals a very special power, obviously founded on divine revelation but also on his own apostolic experience, which confirmed anew the awareness that not wisdom and human eloquence, but only the power of the Holy Spirit builds the Church in the faith (cf. 1 *Co* 1:22-24; 2:4ff.). *Speech*, 21.1.08

Unity and Dialogue between Churches

110. Ecumenical dialogue

This is very important: we must tolerate the separation that exists. St Paul says that divisions are necessary for a certain time and that the Lord knows why: to test us, to train us, to develop us, to make us more humble. But at the same time, we are obliged to move towards unity, and moving towards unity is already a form of unity. *Speech*, 2.3.06

111. Unity

In the first chapter of the Letter to the Christians of Corinth, who were the first to experience the problems and grave temptations of division, we can see a timely message for all Christians. Indeed, a real danger appears when people prefer to identify with one group rather than another, saying, "I belong to Paul" or "I belong to Apollos", or "I belong to Cephas". It was then that Paul asked the searching question. "Is Christ divided?" (1 *Co* 1 13). *Speech*, 14.12.06

112. Need for prayer

"Pray without ceasing" (I *Th* 5:17). St Paul addressed the community of Thessalonica, which was experiencing inner disputes and conflicts, in order to

appeal forcefully for certain fundamental attitudes, among which stands out ceaseless prayer. With this invitation, he wanted to make people understand that the capacity to overcome all selfishness, to live together in peace and fraternal union and for each one to bear the burdens and suffering of others comes from new life in Christ and in the Holy Spirit. We must never tire of praying for Christian unity!
Angelus, 20.1.08

113. Ecumenical relations

The advice that St Paul gave to the Thessalonians can still inspire the behaviour of Christians in the context of ecumenical relations today. Above all he said: "Be at peace among yourselves", and then, "pray constantly, give thanks in all circumstances" (1 *Th* 5:13, 18). Let us also accept the Apostle's pressing exhortation, both to thank the Lord for the progress achieved and to implore full unity.
Catechesis, 23.1.08

Proclaiming the Gospel

114. Preaching

The Apostle of the Gentiles [wrote], that our Saviour "desires all men to be saved and to come to the knowledge of the truth" (1 *Tm* 2:4). This, and nothing else, is the purpose of the Church: the salvation of individual souls. For this reason the Father sent his Son, and in the Lord's own words transmitted to us in the Gospel of Saint John, "as the Father has sent me, even so I send you" (*Jn* 20:21). Hence the mandate to preach the Gospel. *Speech*, 11.5.07

115. The message

The Church's task is none other than to spread the message of Christ, who came, as Saint Paul writes in the Letter to the Ephesians, to proclaim peace to those who are far away and to those who are near (cf. 2:17). *Speech*, 9.1.06

116. Fides ex auditu

Faith, as knowledge and profession of the truth about God and about man, "comes from what is heard, and what is heard comes by the preaching of Christ", as Saint Paul says (*Rm* 10:17). *Homily*, 26.5.06

117. Faith and culture

Christian faith is open to "whatever is true, honourable, just, pure, lovely, gracious" in the culture of peoples, as the Apostle Paul taught the Philippians (cf. 4: 8). *Speech*, 2.6.06

118. Biblical faith and Greek thought

The vision of Saint Paul, who saw the roads to Asia barred and in a dream saw a Macedonian man plead with him: "Come over to Macedonia and help us!" (cf. *Ac* 16:6-10) - this vision can be interpreted as a "distillation" of the intrinsic necessity of a rapprochement between Biblical faith and Greek inquiry. *Speech*, 12.8.06

119. On the Aeropagus

St Paul, at the Aeropagus in Athens... made the first attempt at dialogue with Greek philosophy - and by and large had failed - but they said to him: "We will hear you again". *Catechesis*, 18.4.07

120. Evangelization

The work of evangelization is never a simple adaptation to culture, but it is always also a purification, a courageous break that leads to maturation and healing, an openness that brings to birth that "new creation" (2 *Co* 5:17: *Ga* 6:15) which is the fruit of the Holy Spirit. *Speech*, 19.10.06

121. Faithfulness

To the Lord, whom he first persecuted and then to whom he consecrated his entire being, Paul remains faithful even to death. May his example be an encouragement for all to accept the Word of salvation and translate it into daily life through the faithful following of Christ. *Speech*, 21.1.08

122. Faithfulness

St Paul, it is well-known, originally called by Christ with a personal vocation, was a real Apostle, yet for him too, fidelity to what he received was fundamentally important. He did not want "to invent" a new, so-to-speak, "Pauline" Christianity. Therefore, he insisted, "I have passed on to you what I too received". He passed on the initial gift that comes from the Lord and the truth that saves. Then, towards the end of his life, he wrote to Timothy: "Guard this rich trust with the help of the Holy Spirit that dwells within us (2 *Tm* 1:14). *Catechesis*, 3.5.06

123. Vocation and mission

The story of Paul, the greatest missionary of all time, highlights from a wide range of viewpoints the nexus between vocation and mission. He was accused by his adversaries of not being authorized to be an apostle. However, he repeatedly appeled to his personal vocation, received directly from the Lord (cf. *Rm* 1:1; *Ga* 1:11-12.15.17). *Message*, 3.12.07

124. Peter and Paul

From the outset, Christian tradition has considered Peter and Paul to have been inseparable, even if each had a different mission to accomplish. Peter professed his faith in Christ first; Paul obtained as a gift the ability to deepen its riches. Peter founded the first community of Christians who came from the Chosen People; Paul became the Apostle to the Gentiles. With different charisms they worked for one and the same cause: the building of Christ's Church. *Homily*, 28.6.07

125. Knowledge of Christ

The Church of the third millennium proposes to offer Christians the capacity for "knowledge—according to the words of Saint Paul—of God's mystery, of Christ, in whom are hid all the treasures of wisdom and knowledge" (*Col* 2:2-3). *Speech* (3), 12.5.07

Sacred Ministers

126. Joints of the Church

In his Letter to the Ephesians, St Paul tell us that this Body of Christ, which is the Church, has joints (cf. 4:16) and even names them: they are apostles, prophets, evangelists, pastors and teachers (cf. 4:12). *Homily*, 3.6.07

127. Bishop

By having taken the first few steps in the episcopate you have already realized how necessary it will be to have both humble trust in God and apostolic courage borne of the responsibility of a Bishop. The apostle Paul was aware of this. In front of his pastoral task he put all his hope in the Lord, recognizing that his strength came from him. In fact, he would say: "I can do all in him who gives me strength" (Fil 3.13). Each one of you, dear brothers, must be certain in the unfolding of his ministry that he is never alone, because the lord is close to him with his grace and presence. *Speech*, 19.5.05

128. Mandate

The Risen Lord himself called Paul (cf. *Ga* 1:1), but Paul, although he was called by the Lord to be an Apostle, compared his Gospel with the Gospel of the

Twelve (cf. *ibid.*, 1:18), and was concerned to transmit what he had received (cf. 1 *Co* 11:23; 15:3-4). In the distribution of missionary tasks, he was associated with the Apostles together with others, for example, Barnabas (cf. *Ga* 2:9). Just as becoming an Apostle begins with being called and sent out by the Risen One, so the subsequent call and sending out to others was to be brought about, through the power of the Spirit, by those who are already ordained in the apostolic ministry. *Catechesis*, 10.5.06

129. Priestly portrait

The Apostle Paul's words can apply to us: "Yet preaching the Gospel is not the subject of a boast; I am under compulsion and have no choice. I am ruined if I do not preach it!... Although I am not bound to anyone, I made myself the slave of all so as to win over as many as possible.... I have made myself all things to all men in order to save at least some of them" (1 *Co* 9:16-22). These words that are the self-portrait of the Apostle are also the portrait of every priest. Making oneself "all things to all men" is expressed in daily life, in attention to every person and family *Speech*, 13.5.05

130. Priestly mission

Jesus Christ was sent by the Father, through the power of the Holy Spirit, for the salvation of the entire human family, and we priests are enabled through the grace of the sacrament to share in this mission of his. As the Apostle Paul writes, "God... has given us the ministry of reconciliation.... This makes us ambassadors for Christ, God as it were appealing through us. We implore you, in Christ's name: be reconciled to God" (2 *Co* 5:18-29). This is how St Paul describes our mission as priests. *Speech*, 13.5.05

131. Bearing God

Paul calls Timothy a "man of God" (1 *Tm* 6:11). This is the central task of the priest: to bring God to men and women. Of course, he can only do this if he himself comes from God, if he lives *with* and *by* God. *Speech*, 22.12.06

The Faithful

132. Paul and his collaborators

Paul availed himself of collaborators. He certainly remains the Apostle par excellence, founder and pastor of many Churches. Yet it clearly appears that he did not do everything on his own but relied on trustworthy people who shared in his endeavors and responsibilities... This also seems important to me. Paul does not act as a "soloist", on his own, but together with these collaborators in the "we" of the Church. This "I" of Paul is not an isolated "I" but an "I" in the "we" of the Church, in the "we" of the apostolic faith. *Catechesis*, 13.12.06 and 31.1.07

133. Apostolate

It is necessary to go to the very fringes of society to take to everyone the light of Christ's message about the meaning of life, the family and society, reaching out to those who live in the desert of neglect and poverty and loving them with the love of the Risen Christ. In every apostolate and in Gospel proclamation, as St Paul says, "If I... have not love, I am nothing" (1 *Co* 13:2). *Speech*, 4.7.05

134. Woman in the Church

It is rather to St Paul that we are indebted for a more ample documentation on the dignity and ecclesial role of women. He begins with the fundamental principle according to which for the baptized: "There is neither Jew nor Greek, there is neither slave nor free, there is neither male nor female; for you are all one in Christ Jesus" (*Ga* 3:28), that is, all are united in the same basic dignity, although each with specific functions (cf. 1 *Co* 12:27:30). The Apostle accepts as normal the fact that a woman can "prophesy" in the Christian community (1 *Co* 11:5), that is, speak openly under the influence of the Spirit, as long as it is for the edification of the community and done in a dignified manner.
Catechesis, 14.2.07

135. Humble ministers

Let us think again of St Paul's phrase: both Apollos and I are servants of Jesus, each one in his own way because it is God who gives the growth. These words also apply to us today, to the Pope, the Cardinals, Bishops, priests and laity. We are all humble ministers of Jesus. We serve the Gospel as best we can, in accordance with our talents, and we pray God to make his Gospel, his Church, increase in our day.
Catechesis, 31.1.07

Sacraments

Baptism

136. Pool of regeneration
St Paul tells us: "He saved us, not because of deeds done by us in righteousness, but in virtue of his own mercy, by the washing of regeneration and renewal in the Holy Spirit" (*Ti* 3:5). A washing of regeneration: Baptism is not only a word, it is not only something spiritual but also implies matter. All the realities of the earth are involved. Baptism does not only concern the soul. Human spirituality invests the totality of the person, body and soul. God's action in Jesus Christ is an action of universal efficacy. Christ took flesh and this continues in the sacraments in which matter is taken on and becomes part of the divine action. *Homily*, 7.1.07

137. I, but no longer I
I think that what happens in Baptism can be more easily explained for us if we consider the final part of the short spiritual autobiography that Saint Paul gave us in his Letter to the Galatians. Its concluding words contain the heart of this biography: *"It is no longer I who live, but Christ who lives in me"* (*Ga* 2:20). I live,

but I am no longer I... this phrase is an expression of what happened at Baptism. My "I" is taken away from me and is incorporated into a new and greater subject. This means that my "I" is back again, but now transformed, broken up, opened through incorporation into the other, in whom it acquires its new breadth of existence. *Homily*, 15.4.07

138. New identity

Paul describes the process of his conversion and his Baptism in these words: "it is no longer I who live, but Christ who lives in me" (*Ga* 2:20). Through the coming of the Risen One, Paul obtained a new identity. His closed "I" was opened. Now he lives in communion with Jesus Christ, in the great "I" of believers who have become – as he puts it – "one in Christ" (*Ga* 3:28). *Homily*, 22.3.08

139. With Christ

In Baptism we surrender ourselves, we place our lives in his hands, and so we can say with Saint Paul, "It is no longer I who live, but Christ who lives in me." If we offer ourselves in this way, if we accept, as it were, the death of our very selves, this means that the frontier between death and life is no longer absolute. On either side of death we are with Christ and so, from that moment forward, death is no longer a real boundary. *Homily*, 7.4.07

140. Brothers in Christ

Paul's *Letter to Philemon* is a very personal letter, which Paul wrote from prison and entrusted to the runaway slave Onesimus for his master, Philemon. Yes, Paul is sending the slave back to the master from whom he had fled, not ordering but asking: "I appeal to you for my child ... whose father I have become in my imprisonment ... I am sending him back to you, sending my very heart ... perhaps this is why he was parted from you for a while, that you might have him back for ever, no longer as a slave but more than a slave, as a beloved brother ..." (*Ph* 10-16). Those who, as far as their civil status is concerned, stand in relation to one an other as masters and slaves, inasmuch as they are members of the one Church have become brothers and sisters—this is how Christians addressed one another. By virtue of their Baptism they had been reborn, they had been given to drink of the same Spirit and they received the Body of the Lord together, alongside one another. *Spe salvi*, 4

Eucharistic Reflections

141. Sancta sanctis

In the liturgy of the ancient Church, the distribution of Holy Communion was introduced with the words Sancta sanctis: the holy gift is intended for those who have been made holy. In this way a response was given to the exhortation of St Paul to the Corinthians: "A man should examine himself first; only then should he eat of the bread and drink of the cup..." (1 *Co* 11: 28). *Homily*, 26.5.05

142. Communion

He is the one same Christ who is present in the Eucharistic Bread of every place on earth. This means that we can encounter him only together with all others. We can only receive him in unity. Is not this what the Apostle Paul said in the reading we have just heard? In writing to the Corinthians he said: *"Because the loaf of bread is one, we, many though we are, are one body, for we all partake of the one loaf"* (1 *Co* 10:17). The consequence is clear: we cannot communicate with the Lord if we do not communicate with one another. If we want to present ourselves to him, we must also take a step towards meeting one another. *Homily*, 29.5.05

143. Christ must be seen

Once again, I must return to the Eucharist. "Because there is one bread, we, though many, are one body", says St Paul (1 *Co* 10:17). By this he meant: since we receive the same Lord and he gathers us together and draws us into himself, we ourselves are one. This must be evident in our lives. It must be seen in our capacity to forgive. It must be seen in our sensitivity to the needs of others. It must be seen in our willingness to share. It must be seen in our commitment to our neighbours, both those close at hand and those physically far away, whom we nevertheless consider to be close. *Homily*, 21.8.05

144. Bread of Christ

The bread made up of several grains entails also an event of unity: to become the grains that are grinded is a process of unification. Saint Paul tells us that we ourselves, though many, must become one bread, just one body (1 *Co* 10:17). The sign of bread becomes thus both a sign of hope and a task. *Homily*, 15.6.05

145. Communion

"Because there is one bread, we who are many are one body, for we all partake of the one bread" (1 *Co* 10:17). Union with Christ is also union with all those to whom he gives himself. I cannot possess Christ just for myself; I can belong to him only in union with all those who have become, or who will become, his own. Communion draws me out of myself towards him, and thus also towards unity with all Christians. We become "one body", completely joined in a single existence. *Deus caritas est*, 14

146. Fractio panis
The Apostle of the Gentiles who assures us that, with regard to the Eucharist, he is presenting not his own teaching but what he himself has received (cf. 1 *Co* 11:23). The celebration of the Eucharist implies and involves the living Tradition. The Church celebrates the eucharistic sacrifice in obedience to Christ's command, based on her experience of the Risen Lord and the outpouring of the Holy Spirit. *Sacramentum Caritatis*, 37

147. Christian life as a living sacrifice
Saint Paul's exhortation to the Romans [is] a concise description of how the Eucharist makes our whole life a spiritual worship pleasing to God: "I appeal to you therefore, my brothers, by the mercies of God, to present your bodies as a living sacrifice, holy and acceptable to God, which is your spiritual worship" (*Rm* 12:1). In these words the new worship appears as a total self-offering made in communion with the whole Church. The Apostle's insistence on the offering of our bodies emphasizes the concrete

148. Eucharistic coherence

"Do not be conformed to this world but be transformed by the renewal of your mind, that you may prove what is the will of God, what is good and acceptable and perfect" (12:2). In this way the Apostle of the Gentiles emphasizes the link between true spiritual worship and the need for a new way of understanding and living one's life. An integral part of the eucharistic form of the Christian life is a new way of thinking, "so that we may no longer be children tossed to and fro and carried about with every wind of doctrine" (*Ep* 4:14). *Sacramentum Caritatis*, 77

149. Presence

The Apostle Paul reminded us in his Letter to the Corinthians, that in every Eucharist, also in the Eucharist this evening, we "proclaim the Lord's death until he comes" (cf. 1 *Co* 11:26). We travel on the highways of the world knowing that he is beside us, supported by the hope of being able to see him one day face to face, in the definitive encounter. *Homily*, 7.6.07

Reconciliation

150. Sacrament of reconciliation

Learn, as the Apostle Paul says, to let yourselves be reconciled with God (cf. 2 *Co* 5:20). Especially in the Sacrament of Reconciliation, Jesus waits for you to forgive you your sins and reconcile you with his love through the ministry of the priest. By confessing your sins humbly and truthfully, you will receive the pardon of God himself through the words of his minister. What a great opportunity the Lord has given us with this sacrament to renew ourselves from within and to progress in our Christian life! I recommend that you make good use of it all the time! *Message*, 21.11.05

151. Reconciliation

The Apostle introduces himself as an ambassador of Christ and clearly shows precisely how, in virtue of Christ, the sinner - that is each one of us - is offered the possibility of authentic reconciliation. "For our sakes God made him who did not know sin" he said, "to be sin, so that in him we might become the very holiness of God" (2 *Co* 5:21). Only Christ can transform every situation of sin into newness of grace. *Homily*, 21.2.07

152. Mysterium pietatis

The duty of the priest and the confessor is primarily this: to bring every person to experience the love of Christ, encountering him on the path of their own lives as Paul met him on the road to Damascus. We know the impassioned declaration of the Apostle to the Gentiles after that meeting which changed his life: "[he] loved me and gave himself for me" (*Ga* 2: 20). This is his personal experience on the way to Damascus: the Lord Jesus loved Paul and gave himself for him. And in Confession this is also our way, our way to Damascus, our experience: Jesus has loved me and has given himself for me. *Speech*, 16.3.07

Pray Unceasingly

Prayer in Christian life

153. Prayer
Recalling the words of St Paul: "So neither he who plants nor he who waters is anything, but only God who gives the growth" (1 *Co* 3:7), may we always glimpse through prayer the true source of commitment in charity and by it, verify its authenticity. *Speech*, 21.6.07

154. Pray unceasingly
Paul puts the imperative "pray without ceasing"… the other recommendations would lose their power and coherence were they not sustained by prayer. Unity with God and with others is built first of all through a life of prayer, in the constant search for "the will of God in Christ Jesus for us" (cf. 1 *Th* 5:18). *Homily*, 25.1.08

155. Liturgical prayer
St Paul once said we do not even know what to ask for: "we do not know how to pray as we ought" (Rom 8: 26); we do not know how to pray or what to say to God. God, therefore, has given us words of

prayer in the Psalter, in the important prayers of the Sacred Liturgy, and precisely in the Eucharistic liturgy itself. Here, he teaches us how to pray. We enter into the prayer that was formed down the centuries under the inspiration of the Holy Spirit and we join in Christ's conversation with the Father. Thus, the Liturgy, above all, is prayer: first listening and then a response, in the Responsorial Psalm, in the prayer of the Church and in the great Eucharistic Prayer. *Speech*, 22.2.07

156. Lectio et oratio

It is important to read Sacred Scripture in a very personal way, and really, as St Paul says, not as a human word or a document from the past as we read Homer or Virgil, but as God's Word which is ever timely and speaks to me [cf. 1 *Th* 2,13]. It is important to learn to understand in a historical text, a text from the past, the living Word of God, that is, to enter into prayer and thus read Sacred Scripture as a conversation with God. *Speech*, 17.2.07

157. Lectio divina

The Letter to the Philippians, at the beginning of the great hymn about the Lord, in which the Apostle tells us: "Your attitude must be that of Christ" (*Ph* 2:5), you must enter into the "fronesis", the "fronein", the thinking of Christ... think with Christ's thoughts. And we can do so by reading Sacred Scripture in which Christ's thoughts are the Word, they speak to us. In this sense we must practise "Lectio divina", we must grasp Christ's way of thinking in the Scriptures, we must learn to think with Christ, to think Christ's thoughts and thus feel Christ's sentiments, to be able to convey Christ's thinking to others. *Speech*, 3.10.05

Thoughts on Mary

158. Mother of Jesus

In the Letter to the Galatians St Paul said: "God sent forth his Son, born of woman" (*Ga* 4:4). Origen commented: "Note well that he did not say, 'born by means of a woman' but "born of a woman'" (Comment on the Letter to the Galatians, PG 14, 1298). This acute observation of the great exegete and ecclesiastical writer is important: in fact, if the Son of God had been born only "by means of" a woman, he would not truly have taken on our humanity, something which instead he did by taking flesh "of" Mary. Mary's motherhood, therefore, is true and fully human. The fundamental truth about Jesus as a divine Person who fully assumed our human nature is condensed in the phrase: "God sent forth his Son born of woman". He is the Son of God, he is generated by God and at the same time he is the son of a woman, Mary. He comes from her. He is of God and of Mary. For this reason one can and must call the Mother of Jesus the Mother of God. *Homily*, 31.12.06

159. Our mother

St Paul very discreetly mentions the One through whom the Son of God entered the world: "when the time had fully come", he wrote, "God sent forth his

Son, born of woman" (*Ga* 4:4). The Church contemplates in the "woman" the features of Mary of Nazareth, a unique woman because she was called to carry out a mission that brought her into very close contact with Christ: indeed, it was an absolutely unique relationship, because Mary is Mother of the Savior. Just as obviously, however, we can and must affirm that she is our Mother because, by living her very special maternal relationship with the Son, she shared in his mission *for us* and *for the salvation of all people*. Homily, 31.12.07

A world of Catholic reading at your fingertips ...

CTS

... now online
Browse 500 titles at
www.cts-online.org.uk

Catholic Faith, Life, and Truth for all   **CTS**